I0415794

January 2012

ENDANGERED SEA TURTLES

Better Coordination, Data Collection, and Planning Could Improve Federal Protection and Recovery Efforts

G A O
Accountability * Integrity * Reliability

GAO-12-242

January 2012

ENDANGERED SEA TURTLES

Better Coordination, Data Collection, and Planning Could Improve Federal Protection and Recovery Efforts

Why GAO Did This Study

All six species of sea turtles found in U.S. waters and nesting on U.S. shores are listed as endangered under the Endangered Species Act. Two federal agencies—the National Marine Fisheries Service (NMFS) and the Fish and Wildlife Service (FWS)—are charged with protecting sea turtles, NMFS when the turtles are at sea and FWS on land. The act prohibits the "take," including harassment or killing, of protected species. The services (NMFS and FWS) can, however, authorize take under certain circumstances. The act also requires recovery plans for each listed species, which set forth broad goals and recovery strategies. GAO was asked to determine the extent to which the services (1) coordinate their sea turtle protection activities, (2) collect and analyze take data, (3) clearly explain how they determine if a proposed action will jeopardize sea turtles, and (4) have developed operational plans to help realize recovery goals. To address these issues, GAO reviewed documents and interviewed officials from both services and experts, including state agency officials, university researchers, and representatives of environmental and industry groups.

What GAO Recommends

GAO is making four recommendations to the Secretaries of Commerce and the Interior to improve the services' sea turtle coordination, data collection, reporting, and planning efforts. Both NMFS and FWS generally agreed with the recommendations.

View GAO-12-242. For more information, contact Anu K. Mittal at (202) 512-3841 or mittala@gao.gov.

What GAO Found

The services have coordinated some sea turtle protection efforts, including jointly developing recovery plans, and they established a memorandum of understanding in 1977 to define their roles in joint administration of their efforts. Nevertheless, neither the memorandum nor the services have clearly defined how and when the services are to coordinate; also, the services do not consistently share information about the majority of the take they authorize. According to sea turtle experts GAO spoke with, each service may therefore be authorizing sea turtle take without knowing how much its counterpart has authorized, and the combined allowance may be harming threatened and endangered sea turtles and delaying their recovery.

NMFS and FWS each use databases that collect information about consultations involving take of sea turtles and other species, but they do not use these databases to comprehensively collect and analyze sea turtle take data. Specifically, not all of the databases require entry of data on anticipated and actual take. The services also maintain separate documents that collect information about anticipated take, but these documents are not structured to easily allow analysis of total anticipated take and do not track actual take. According to some experts and NMFS officials GAO spoke with, total take should be considered when the services determine whether proposed actions are likely to jeopardize species or approve additional take authorizations.

Biological opinions prepared by NMFS and FWS do not clearly explain how the services determine that an action anticipated to result in the take of sea turtles will not jeopardize their continued existence. Guidance developed by the services states that the opinions should be written so the general public can trace the path of logic to the conclusion. But some experts GAO spoke with said, and GAO's review of selected biological opinions found, that the opinions may not clearly describe why the services conclude that a particular action, such as commercial fishing anticipated to harm turtles, will not jeopardize the species' existence. If the analyses and decisions in the opinions are not clear, neither Congress nor the public can be assured that the services are adequately protecting vulnerable sea turtle populations as required by the Endangered Species Act.

Neither NMFS nor FWS has developed its own service-specific operational plans describing the actions it will perform to achieve the goals in their jointly prepared sea turtle recovery plans. In the absence of service-specific plans, the services rely on the jointly developed recovery plans to guide their sea turtle protection and recovery efforts. But GAO's review of these recovery plans found that they do not include key elements of effective planning, such as performance measures to gauge progress toward goals. Without service-specific plans and performance measures, neither service can ensure that it is taking the steps needed to realize sea turtle recovery goals.

Contents

Abbreviations

FWS   Fish and Wildlife Service
NMFS   National Marine Fisheries Service
NOAA   National Oceanic and Atmospheric Administration

This is a work of the U.S. government and is not subject to copyright protection in the United States. The published product may be reproduced and distributed in its entirety without further permission from GAO. However, because this work may contain copyrighted images or other material, permission from the copyright holder may be necessary if you wish to reproduce this material separately.

United States Government Accountability Office
Washington, DC 20548

January 31, 2012

The Honorable Sheldon Whitehouse
Chairman
Subcommittee on Oversight
Committee on Environment and Public Works
United States Senate

The Honorable Sam Farr
House of Representatives

Sea turtles—ancient, highly migratory reptiles—today number worldwide just a small percentage of their populations from a century ago. Although six species are still found in the waters or on the beaches of the United States, all six—green, hawksbill, Kemp's ridley, leatherback, loggerhead, and olive ridley—are listed as endangered in all or part of their range[1] under the Endangered Species Act.[2] These sea turtle species have been protected under the act since the 1970s, but no species has recovered to an extent that would allow its removal from the list of protected species or a change in its status from endangered to threatened.

Sea turtles inhabit both ocean and land environments, and two federal agencies are charged with protecting them under the act. Sea turtles spend most of their lives in the open ocean, but female sea turtles must return to land to lay their eggs. Sea turtles are vulnerable to a number of threats, both at sea and on land. Some of these threats are the result of human-caused actions, including unintentional injury or death due to

---

[1]Range refers to the geographic area a species is known or believed to occupy.

[2]16 U.S.C. §§ 1531-1544 (2006). Under the Endangered Species Act, "endangered species" is defined, generally, as "any species which is in danger of extinction throughout all or a significant portion of its range," and "threatened species" is defined as "any species which is likely to become an endangered species within the foreseeable future throughout all or a significant portion of its range." 16 U.S.C. § 1532(6), (20) (2006). Certain populations of green, loggerhead, and olive ridley turtles are listed separately as threatened.

(1) fishing in state, federal, and international waters;[3] (2) environmental contamination from events such as oil spills; or (3) loss or degradation of nesting habitat through beachfront development. Two federal agencies—the Department of Commerce's National Marine Fisheries Service (NMFS), within the National Oceanic and Atmospheric Administration (NOAA), and the Department of the Interior's Fish and Wildlife Service (FWS)—share the responsibility for managing the conservation and recovery of sea turtles.[4] NMFS is specifically responsible for managing sea turtle populations in the marine environment, and FWS is specifically responsible for managing them on land.[5] Each service has multiple regional or field offices that carry out sea turtle protection in particular geographic areas.

The Endangered Species Act provides direction for conserving threatened and endangered species, including sea turtles. Specifically, section 9 of the act generally prohibits the "take" of endangered species. The act defines take as "to harass, harm, pursue, hunt, shoot, wound, kill, trap, capture, or collect, or to attempt to engage in any such conduct."[6] Under section 7 of the act, federal agencies must ensure that any action they authorize, fund, or carry out is unlikely to jeopardize the continued existence of a listed species or destroy or adversely modify its critical habitat.[7] To fulfill this responsibility, federal agencies must consult with the services when their actions may affect listed species or critical habitat. Formal consultations generally result in the issuance by the applicable service of reports known as "biological opinions," which discuss in detail the effects of proposed actions on listed species and their critical habitat,

---

[3]State waters generally extend from the shore to 3 nautical miles offshore. Federal waters, which are waters under the jurisdiction of the federal government, generally extend from 3 nautical miles to 200 nautical miles offshore. Waters beyond 200 nautical miles offshore are considered international waters.

[4]Throughout this report, we refer to NMFS and FWS as "the services."

[5]Authority for sea turtle management has been delegated by the Secretary of Commerce to NMFS's Assistant Administrator for Fisheries and by the Secretary of the Interior to the Director of FWS. Throughout this report, we refer to requirements on the Secretaries as requirements on the services.

[6]16 U.S.C. § 1532(19) (2006).

[7]Throughout this report, the term "listed species" includes not only the species itself but also its critical habitat, if critical habitat has been designated under the Endangered Species Act.

as well as that service's opinion on whether a proposed action is likely to jeopardize a species' continued existence or destroy or adversely modify its critical habitat. The opinion also determines the quantity or extent of anticipated "incidental take"—that is, take that is not intentional but occurs nonetheless as a result of carrying out an agency action. The act generally requires development of "recovery plans" for each listed species, which set forth goals, criteria, and actions to guide the services' recovery efforts. The act also requires certain entities, such as scientists engaged in research on listed species or landowners engaged in activity likely to cause the incidental take of a listed species, to obtain a permit from the appropriate service.

You asked us to investigate the degree of coordination between NMFS and FWS related to sea turtle protection and take determinations. Accordingly, this report examines the extent to which the two services (1) coordinate their sea turtle protection activities, (2) collect and analyze data on anticipated and actual sea turtle take, (3) clearly explain in their biological opinions the rationales they use when determining whether a proposed action will jeopardize sea turtles, and (4) have developed operational plans to help realize the goals of recovery plans for sea turtle species.

We addressed these objectives by taking a variety of steps. Specifically, we reviewed the memorandum of understanding between NMFS and FWS regarding their sea turtle protection activities. We also reviewed the information contained in four databases the services use to collect information on anticipated and actual take of sea turtles. We reviewed all 22 of the biological opinions issued from January 1, 2006, to January 1, 2011, by NMFS for federal fisheries and a random sample consisting of 21 of the 119 biological opinions issued by FWS for the same time period that included actions anticipated to result in the take of sea turtles.[8] Additionally, we reviewed all of the sea turtle recovery plans and other related plans developed by the services. To gain a national perspective on sea turtle protection efforts, we interviewed NMFS's and FWS's

---

[8]The term "fishery" means one or more stocks of fish that can be treated as a unit for purposes of conservation and management and that are identified on the basis of geographic, scientific, technical, recreational, and economic characteristics. We use the term "federal fishery" to mean a fishery managed by the regional fishery management councils and NMFS. The councils are composed of federal and state fishery management officials, as well as active fishery participants, among others, and are responsible for developing management plans for fisheries in federal waters.

national sea turtle coordinators and officials with national sea turtle protection responsibilities. We also interviewed a range of experts and other individuals—including university researchers; representatives of nongovernmental organizations, such as Oceana; and representatives from regional fishery management councils—whom we identified as knowledgeable about national sea turtle protection efforts. To examine the services' sea turtle protection efforts in greater depth, and to better understand any regional differences, we gathered information for four states: Florida, Hawaii, Massachusetts, and Texas. We selected these states primarily because of their sea turtle nesting populations, federally managed fisheries offshore, and a relatively high level of anticipated take associated with these fishing operations. For these four states, we analyzed documentation and interviewed a diverse range of individuals involved in sea turtle protection, including the services' regional and field office officials; other federal and state agency officials; and experts from industry, such as the Southern Shrimp Alliance, and from environmental groups, such as the Sea Turtle Conservancy. Appendix I discusses our scope and methodology in more detail.

We conducted this performance audit from February 2011 to January 2012, in accordance with generally accepted government auditing standards. Those standards require that we plan and perform the audit to obtain sufficient, appropriate evidence to provide a reasonable basis for our findings and conclusions based on our audit objectives. We believe that the evidence obtained provides a reasonable basis for our findings and conclusions based on our audit objectives.

Background

The purpose of the Endangered Species Act is to conserve threatened and endangered species, including sea turtles, and the ecosystems on which they depend. The act provides for listing species that need protection; designating habitat deemed critical to a listed species' conservation; protecting listed species against certain harms caused by federal and nonfederal actions; conducting 5-year reviews on species' status; and developing recovery plans that contain objective, measurable criteria that, when met, would result in a determination that the species can be removed from the list.

Among provisions in the act, section 9 generally prohibits the take of listed endangered animal species.[9] The act, however, also provides for key exceptions to section 9's take prohibition. Specifically:

- Section 10, among other things, provides an avenue for entities to obtain permits for activities that may result in the take of listed species:

  - Under section 10(a)(1)(A), the services can issue permits for take resulting from scientific research or actions to enhance the propagation or survival of a listed species.

  - Under section 10(a)(1)(B), the services can issue "incidental take permits" for incidental take by nonfederal entities, such as take anticipated from states' permitting construction on a beach.

- Section 7 directs federal agencies to consult with the services when these agencies determine that an action they authorize, fund, or carry out could affect listed species.[10] Formal consultation is required unless the action agency finds, with either NMFS's or FWS's written concurrence, that a proposed action is not likely to adversely affect the species. To initiate a formal consultation, an action agency submits to the appropriate service a written request describing the proposed action and its likely effects on the listed species and its habitat. The consultation usually ends with NMFS or FWS issuing a biological opinion.

Example of consultation under section 7

To comply with section 7 of the Endangered Species Act, if an "action agency" such as the U.S. Army Corps of Engineers (Corps) wants to replenish the sand on a beach where sea turtles nest, it must consult with FWS because this action could bury sea turtle nests or kill mature females and hatchlings. If FWS determines that this project is not likely to jeopardize the continued existence of the sea turtle species in question, it must issue an incidental take statement, which specifies the impact of anticipated take and sets conditions for minimizing it. If the Corps adheres to these conditions, any take incidental to the project is excepted from the provision in the act that prohibits take. Nevertheless, take in excess of what is anticipated triggers reinitiation of consultation between the action agency and the applicable service.

---

[9]Section 4(d) of the act authorizes the services to extend the prohibition against take to threatened species. Both services have done so with respect to threatened sea turtle species.

[10]Section 7 also applies to the services' own activities, including issuing section 10 permits to nonfederal parties; in such cases, the service conducts an "intraservice" consultation.

Both take permits and take statements describe the take that has been authorized and specify the conditions under which it may occur.[11] Take is generally expressed as the number of individuals of a species killed or injured, except in circumstances where this number would be difficult to determine or monitor. In these instances, a substitute measure of the species resource loss is used, such as the miles of beach expected to be affected. In addition, a section 7 take statement specifies "reasonable and prudent measures," that is, steps that may minimize the impact to the species of any take anticipated to occur. An incidental take permit is conditioned upon an applicant's submission of a habitat conservation plan that specifies steps the applicant will take to minimize and mitigate anticipated take. For example, an action may be restricted to a time of year when the species is not present, buffer zones might be required around known nesting areas, or species might have to be trapped and moved elsewhere before an action can proceed. A habitat conservation plan is not required to obtain a scientific research permit, but the services' regulations subject such permits to various conditions as well.

The services' biological opinions, which are to be based on "the best scientific and commercial data available," constitute the services' determinations as to whether the effects of an action, when viewed against a species' status, are likely to jeopardize that species' continued existence. In their biological opinions, the services are to evaluate, among other things, a species' current status, its "environmental baseline,"[12] and the effects on the species of the action, including the quantity or extent of incidental take that service biologists anticipate will result from the action. Actual take occurring as a result of an action could be higher or lower

---

[11]Through permits issued under section 10, the services formally authorize the taking of listed species. Under section 7, however, the services do not formally authorize the taking of listed species by federal agencies; rather, they consult with federal entities on their proposed actions. While federal agencies are shielded from the act's take prohibition if they comply with the conditions set out in an incidental take statement, they do not need the services' permission to proceed with an action. Nevertheless, because an incidental take statement has the same practical effect as a take authorization associated with section 10 permits—that is, an incidental take statement effectively authorizes incidental take—for simplicity, we refer generally to "authorized take" or "anticipated take" when discussing take in the context of both sections 7 and 10.

[12]To determine the environmental baseline, the services analyze the effects of past and present human and natural factors leading to a species' current status, its habitat, and ecosystem within the action area. The environmental baseline includes the impacts of all federal, state, or private actions—including the anticipated impacts of all proposed federal actions in the area—that have already undergone separate consultation with the services.

than the anticipated estimate. Biological opinions also contain provisions directing the action agency to monitor the action's effects on listed species and to reenter into, or reinitiate, consultation if the quantity or extent of anticipated take is exceeded.

In addition, section 4 of the Endangered Species Act requires the services to develop and implement recovery plans for the conservation and survival of threatened and endangered species, unless the services determine that a plan will not promote their conservation. The act directs the services, to the maximum extent practicable, to incorporate in each recovery plan (1) a description of site-specific management actions necessary to achieve the plan's goal for the conservation and survival of the species; (2) objective, measurable criteria that will result in a determination that the species can be removed from the list of threatened and endangered species; and (3) estimates of the time and cost required to carry out those actions needed to achieve the plan's goal and to achieve intermediate steps toward the goal. Recovery teams, which may include independent scientists and experts, can be formed to advise and assist the services in developing and implementing recovery plans. Section 4 of the act also requires the services to review the status of each listed species at least once every 5 years to determine whether any species should be removed from the list, changed from endangered to threatened, or changed from threatened to endangered.

NMFS and FWS have divided their responsibilities for sea turtle protection among their respective staff located in headquarters and regional and field offices. Both services have established national sea turtle coordinators to oversee each service's activities, with NMFS's national coordinator located in headquarters in the Washington, D.C., area and FWS's national coordinator located in its Jacksonville, Florida, field office. Both services' headquarters also have staff responsible for implementing various aspects of the Endangered Species Act, although these staff may have other responsibilities in addition to sea turtle protection. In addition, each service has a network of regional or field offices with sea turtle protection responsibilities, which coordinate with other offices within the service when necessary. For example, NMFS relies primarily on four regional offices (Northeast, Pacific Islands, Southeast, and Southwest) to issue sea turtle section 7 take statements and lead other protection efforts. In each of these four regions, NMFS also has fisheries science centers that conduct research on marine resources, including sea turtles. Similarly, FWS has multiple regional and field offices with responsibility for sea turtle protection efforts. Unlike NMFS's oversight, however, FWS's oversight of sea turtles falls primarily under the purview of its Southeast and Southwest regional offices and a few field offices—in particular, its North Florida Ecological Services Office in Jacksonville—in part because most sea turtle nesting in the United States takes place on beaches in the Southeast. According to officials from both services and representatives of external parties whom we spoke with, the regional and field offices from both services also work with external parties, such as state agencies, industry, and nongovernmental organizations, on sea turtle protection activities.

NMFS and FWS Coordinate on Some but Not All Take Decisions

The services have coordinated with each other on some but not all of their take authorizations, even though experts have pointed out the importance of such coordination when assessing threats to sea turtle species. Given the services' joint administrative responsibilities for protecting sea turtles under the Endangered Species Act, a memorandum of understanding was established that defined those responsibilities and called for coordination of certain activities. This memorandum, however, has not been updated since it went into effect in 1977 and lacks clarity on several points.

We found that the services coordinate some of their activities when deciding whether to authorize sea turtle take. For example:

- The services have sometimes coordinated before issuing or denying permits under section 10(a)(1)(A) of the Endangered Species Act. Specifically, NMFS officials told us that before issuing science and research permits, they routinely consult with FWS or the states, unless the proposed action is expected to occur solely in federal waters. Similarly, FWS officials told us that when deciding whether to permit facilities for sea turtle rehabilitation, they have also coordinated with NMFS by consulting with the coordinator of NMFS's sea turtle stranding program and with NMFS's sea turtle veterinarian regarding the best care for the species.[13]

---

[13]NMFS coordinates the Sea Turtle Stranding and Salvage Network, which operates in most coastal regions of the United States. The network was established in 1980 to collect information on and document strandings of sea turtles and includes federal, state, and private partners. NMFS defines strandings as turtles that wash ashore, dead or alive, or are found floating dead or in a weakened condition.

Kemp's ridley *(Lepidochelys kempii)*

Source: NPS photo.

Smallest of the sea turtles, an adult Kemp's ridley weighs up to 100 pounds and has a shell averaging about 2 feet long. Found mainly in the Gulf of Mexico, Kemp's ridleys reach sexual maturity at 7 to 15 years of age. The adults are bottom-feeders with a taste for crabs; juveniles have been known to find refuge and food in floating seaweed, such as *Sargassum*. Kemp's ridley is one of two sea turtle species to nest in massive events known as *arribadas*, where thousands of females come ashore in daylight to nest on the same beach at the same time; an estimated 40,000 or more females came ashore in Tamaulipas, Mexico, on a single day in 1947. By 1985, the number of nests worldwide had dropped to 702, with fewer than 400 nesting females. Intensive conservation efforts have helped put the species on a more positive trajectory, although the number of strandings has notably increased in the Gulf of Mexico since May 2010. The species has been listed under the Endangered Species Act since 1970 as endangered.

• For section 7 take statements, officials from both services told us that they work together if an action is expected to affect sea turtles both on land and in marine environments. Such coordination typically occurs in the services' regional or field offices. For example, FWS officials told us that they coordinate with NMFS officials for land-based projects that may also have in-water components, such as breakwaters.[14]

In contrast, we also found instances where the services have not coordinated or shared take information before making take decisions. For example:

• According to NMFS officials we spoke with, for incidental take permits issued under section 10(a)(1)(B), NMFS has not coordinated on all permit applications in the past.[15] NMFS officials also told us, however, that they are currently coordinating with FWS on an application for gillnet fishing in state waters in North Carolina.[16] Similarly, FWS officials told us that they do not send NMFS applications for either type of section 10 permit for review and comment before issuance. The officials also told us that they solicit public comments via the *Federal Register*, which can include comments from local, state, and federal agencies.[17]

• With regard to section 7 take statements, if an action is expected to fall solely within the purview of one service, which is typically the case, officials from both services told us that they generally do not coordinate or share take information before issuing the take statement. Coordination on section 7 take statements is important, officials from both services told us, because such take constitutes the majority of authorized sea turtle take and, for NMFS, represents the majority of lethal take. In some instances, however, coordination

---

[14]Breakwaters are structures placed offshore to reduce the amount of wave energy reaching a protected area.

[15]In commenting on a draft of this report, NOAA stated that to date NMFS has issued only four section 10(a)(1)(B) permits, three of which are still active. Similarly, FWS officials told us that FWS has issued few section 10(a)(1)(B) permits.

[16]Gillnets are large, rectangular, mesh nets that can entangle sea turtles, preventing them from surfacing for air and thereby drowning them.

[17]The Endangered Species Act requires both services to seek such comments.

GAO-12-242 Endangered Sea Turtles

between the services does occur. For example, officials from NMFS's Pacific Islands Regional Office told us that they coordinate closely with FWS and also send FWS copies of all section 7 consultations. FWS officials told us that they recently coordinated with NMFS by requesting comments from NMFS officials on a draft programmatic biological opinion. The opinion, developed under section 7, applies to all sand placement projects in Florida, including beach nourishment activities, initiated after the opinion was finalized in 2011. According to the officials, such projects account for approximately 90 percent of the biological opinions the service develops for sea turtles.

University researchers and representatives of nongovernmental organizations we spoke with told us that coordination between NMFS and FWS on section 10 take permits and section 7 take statements is important because each service should consider take anticipated by the other service when assessing threats to sea turtle populations as part of the jeopardy determination process. Specifically, some of these experts told us that such coordination is necessary because both services are issuing take statements and permits that can affect a given single species of sea turtle. As a result, each service should consider all threats to that species, regardless of whether such threats occur on land or at sea.[18] Moreover, a handbook jointly developed by the services emphasizes the importance of coordination between NMFS and FWS, stating that coordination is "critical" when developing section 7 consultations.

Our prior work has also shown the importance of coordination and information sharing. For example, we found that without coordination among federal agencies with fragmented or overlapping programs, scarce funds are wasted, program customers are confused and frustrated, and the overall effectiveness of the federal effort is limited.[19] Our work has

---

[18]The services must examine the current status of the species across its entire range, as well as the environmental baseline of the species within the action area, to make a jeopardy determination. Rock Creek Alliance v. United States Fish & Wildlife Service, 390 F. Supp. 2d 993, 1010 (D. Mont. 2005). Even within the action area, however, the services are not necessarily required to numerically add together all sources of take anticipated by other activities. Oceana, Inc. v. Evans, 384 F. Supp. 2d 203, 230-231 (D.D.C. 2005). Experts we spoke with, however, agreed that tallying anticipated take is an important tool available to the services as they consider what activities may threaten the continued existence of sea turtles.

[19]GAO, *Managing for Results: Barriers to Interagency Coordination*, GAO/GGD-00-106 (Washington, D.C.: Mar. 29, 2000).

Hawksbill *(Eretmochelys imbricata)*

Source: Caroline Rogers, U.S. Geological Survey.

Named after a distinctive hawklike beak at the tip of its head, the relatively small adult hawksbill sea turtle weighs from 95 to 165 pounds and has a shell averaging about 2.5 feet long. Hawksbills feed primarily on sponges, which they pry from crevices with their beaks. In contrast to all other sea turtle species, hawksbill females nest in low densities on scattered, typically small beaches in the tropics. Hawksbill turtles have been exploited for hundreds of years as the source of commercial tortoiseshell, and despite global restrictions, a significant illegal trade continues. Since 1970, the species has been listed under the Endangered Species Act as endangered.

also shown that information sharing is a key practice for enhancing and sustaining collaboration.[20] Because the services are not consistently sharing information on anticipated take, they may be making jeopardy determinations about sea turtle species without knowing how much take the counterpart service has authorized, and the combined take may be harming threatened and endangered sea turtles and delaying their recovery.

Given the services' joint administrative responsibilities for sea turtle protection, the services in 1977 established a memorandum of understanding to define their roles. The memorandum calls for the services to coordinate on certain activities, including consulting with the other service before publishing regulations, establishing recovery teams, and issuing or denying "permits." Officials from both services told us they have coordinated on some activities as called for in the memorandum, which is still in effect. For example, the national sea turtle coordinators from both services jointly lead efforts to develop recovery plans.

We found, however, that the memorandum of understanding is outdated and has not been updated to reflect changes in the services' sea turtle protection efforts. For example, we found that the memorandum calls only for consultation on "permits," which, according to officials from both services, would imply that it applies only to permits described under sections 10(a)(1)(A) and 10(a)(1)(B) of the Endangered Species Act and therefore does not call for coordination on section 7 take statements, even though actions under section 7 account for the majority of sea turtle take. According to an FWS official, this limitation of the memorandum may reflect the fact that section 7 take statements were not part of the process until amendments to the act in 1982, whereas the memorandum was signed in 1977. In addition, the memorandum designates FWS's Federal Wildlife Permit Office as a clearinghouse to retain all applications for sea turtle permits or certifications; according to an FWS official, however, FWS no longer has such a clearinghouse.

Moreover, the memorandum of understanding is unclear on the nature and degree of coordination the services are to engage in. Specifically, we found the following areas where the memorandum was unclear:

[20]GAO, *Results-Oriented Government: Practices That Can Help Enhance and Sustain Collaboration among Federal Agencies*, GAO-06-15 (Washington, D.C.: Oct. 21, 2005).

- The memorandum does not clearly articulate the coordination-related steps each service is to take before issuing or denying take permits. For example, the memorandum does not lay out whether a service should share information on take it has previously permitted for a particular species; neither does the memorandum state whether a service should provide the other service a copy of take requests it receives or if it is sufficient for the services to simply notify each other that a request has been received.

- The memorandum does not explain at what stages of the take permitting process such coordination should occur. For example, the memorandum does not specify if the services should coordinate (1) upon receipt of a request for a permit for activity anticipated to result in take, (2) when analysis within a service is initiated, or (3) after a service has completed its evaluation of a permit application.

- The memorandum leaves room for interpretation by each service on what degree of coordination is required. For example, according to FWS officials, they interpret the memorandum as calling for general cooperation, not necessarily for coordination with NMFS on all the specific activities laid out in the memorandum.

Even though the memorandum of understanding is out of date and unclear, neither service has developed formal guidance to supplement the memorandum or has offered any plans to update it. Without clear language and agreement about what degree of coordination is expected of each service, it is unlikely that consistent, meaningful coordination will occur.

Neither Service Uses Its Section 7 and Section 10 Databases to Comprehensively Collect and Analyze Data on Anticipated or Actual Take

NMFS and FWS each maintain databases that contain information about take consultations for sea turtles and other species under section 7 of the Endangered Species Act and take permits under sections 10(a)(1)(A) and 10(a)(1)(B). Not all of these databases, however, require entry of anticipated or actual take data, and the services do not use them to analyze sea turtle take. Instead, the services' national sea turtle coordinators have developed their own documents for collecting anticipated take information, although they have not systematically used them to analyze total take. Our prior work has shown a need for tracking total take information,[21] but the services do not plan to update their databases to add such capability.

NMFS maintains the following two databases to collect consultation information and some sea turtle take data:

- In NMFS's Authorizations and Permits for Protected Species database, NMFS staff are required to enter information about take anticipated from permits primarily for scientific research or actions to enhance propagation or survival of a listed species under the Endangered Species Act's section 10(a)(1)(A).[22] Through the use of this database, NMFS collects a number of details about anticipated take for scientific research permits, including the species and sex of animals to be taken. For example, the database may show that 25 juvenile green sea turtles are expected to be captured and released during an activity designed to tag and weigh the turtles and take blood samples. Permittees may directly enter actual take data into the database if they submit the data online to NMFS, but they may also submit such data in writing to NMFS staff. As a result, a NMFS official told us, the database has incomplete data on actual take, although, other officials also told us, for section 10(a)(1)(A) and 10(a)(1)(B) permits, they have other sources of actual take data that are not stored in the database.

---

[21]GAO, *Endangered Species Act: The U.S. Fish and Wildlife Service Has Incomplete Information about Effects on Listed Species from Section 7 Consultations*, GAO-09-550 (Washington, D.C.: May 21, 2009).

[22]The database also contains limited data on incidental take anticipated by permits for nonfederal entities under section 10(a)(1)(B) of the act, but entry of anticipated and actual take data is not required, nor is such take tracked.

Green sea turtle *(Chelonia mydas)*

Source: Andy Bruckner, National Oceanic and Atmospheric Administration.

With a shell (carapace) 3 to 4 feet long and a total weight of 300 to 350 pounds, green sea turtles are unique among marine turtles in that they are almost exclusively plant eating (herbivorous). They take their name from the color of their fat, whose green tint is thought to come from the adult turtles' diet of sea grasses and algae. After reaching sexual maturity at anywhere from 20 to 50 years of age, female turtles return every 2 to 4 years to the same beaches where they were hatched. The two largest nesting populations are found on Tortuguero, on the Caribbean coast of Costa Rica, where some 22,500 females nest per season, and Raine Island on Australia's Great Barrier Reef, where 18,000 females are known to nest per season on average. On U.S. shores, green turtles nest primarily along the coasts of Florida and Hawaii, which may each harbor an estimated 200 to as many as 1,100 females annually. Green turtles were first listed under the Endangered Species Act in 1978. Breeding populations in Florida and on the Pacific coast of Mexico are listed as endangered; all other populations are listed as threatened.

- NMFS's Public Consultation Tracking System is used to store data on proposed actions by federal agencies consulting with NMFS under section 7. Although the database has a narrative field for anticipated take data, and staff can use a drop-down menu to label the anticipated take as either lethal or injurious, NMFS has no requirement for staff to enter this information into the database, and the database does not have a field for capturing actual take data. As a result, a NMFS official told us, some regions consistently enter take data into this database, and others do not.

FWS also maintains the following two databases to collect consultation information and some take data:

- FWS's Service Permit Issuance and Tracking System stores information about take anticipated by both types of take permits issued under section 10. As a result of an October 2011 update making entry of such data mandatory, FWS staff are now required to enter anticipated take data into this system. Although the October 2011 update will help ensure that the information entered into the database is more complete, it will still not be comprehensive, in part because FWS's Region 5, which covers the northeastern United States, does not use the database for all of its permits, and the database does not have a field for capturing actual take data.

- FWS's Tracking and Integrated Logging System is used to collect information about actions potentially resulting in the take of sea turtles by federal agencies consulting with FWS under section 7. It is optional, however, for agency staff to enter anticipated and actual take data into this database, and the information is entered in a narrative form, so data are not entered in a consistent format. For example, some entries list miles of beach expected to be affected, while others instead list the number of turtles and nests expected to be taken. In commenting on a draft of this report, Interior officials said it is not possible to determine the exact number of individual sea turtles that would be taken during actions such as beach nourishment projects because the number of nests on a beach varies annually and the exact number of nests missed during surveys cannot be known. In addition, the officials questioned the value of "standardized" data."

In part because of differences in the collection and types of take data in the services' databases, we found that the services generally do not use their databases to systematically analyze anticipated and actual take. NMFS officials told us, however, that for section 10 permits, because they have some take data in the Authorizations and Permits for Protected Species database—as well as some data from sources outside the database, such as the Public Consultation Tracking System and published and unpublished literature—they analyze anticipated and actual take using the database in combination with these other data sources.

In the absence of servicewide databases that comprehensively capture anticipated take data, both services' national sea turtle coordinators maintain documents that collect information about anticipated take. These documents, however, are not structured to easily allow—nor have the services provided us clear evidence that they have used them for—analyzing total anticipated take. For example, NMFS has spreadsheets with fields, by species, where data on anticipated lethal and nonlethal take may be entered. According to NMFS officials we spoke with, because section 10 take permits and section 7 take statements can authorize take for a single year or over multiple years, some of these data are in a per-year format, while other data cover several years. In addition, some data fields contain both numbers and text, making it difficult to analyze or calculate total anticipated take.[23] As a result, NMFS officials told us that it can be difficult to analyze total take using these spreadsheets. Moreover, the spreadsheets do not track actual take, and therefore NMFS cannot use these spreadsheets to analyze actual take data. Furthermore, while some officials stated they had access to these spreadsheets, others did not have access. For example, some NMFS officials told us that these spreadsheets were regularly provided to regional officials and used in section 7 consultations. During our review, however, other NMFS officials told us that the spreadsheets were not made available to them. In particular, one regional biologist told us he

[23]A congressional committee that in 1982 was considering amendments to the Endangered Species Act indicated that the committee preferred the incidental take statement to contain a numerical value: "[W]here possible, the impact should be specified in terms of a numerical limitation on the federal agency or permittee or licensee." The committee recognized, however, that a numerical value would not always be available: "The Committee recognizes . . . it may not be possble to determine the number of eggs of an endangered or threatened fish which will be sucked into a power plant when water is used as a cooling mechanism. The Committee intends only that such numbers be established where possible." H.R. Rep. No. 97-567, at 27 (1982). In 2007, the U.S. Court of Appeals for the Ninth Circuit ruled that if the service chooses to employ a nonnumerical surrogate for take, the chosen surrogate must be able to perform the functions of a numerical limitation, in particular, establishing a trigger requiring the parties to reinitiate consultation. Oregon Natural Resources Council v. Allen, 476 F.3d 1031, 1038 (9th Cir. 2007).

Leatherback *(Dermochelys coriacea)*

Source: Scott R. Benson, NMFS Southwest Fisheries Science Center.

Leatherbacks are the largest, deepest-diving, and widest-ranging of all sea turtle species, reaching an adult length of up to 8 feet and weighing up to 2,000 pounds. Unlike other sea turtles, and as their name suggests, leatherbacks are not hard shelled; rather, their carapaces consist of leathery, oil-saturated connective tissue on top of loosely interlocking bones within the skin. They are also unusual among reptiles because they can maintain their body temperature, an adaptation enabling them to migrate into colder water than other sea turtles, following swarms of jellyfish that are their primary prey. Leatherbacks reach sexual maturity at ages 6 to 10, and nesting takes place in the tropics and subtropics, normally at night. Leatherbacks have been listed since 1970 under the Endangered Species Act as endangered.

was not aware that anticipated sea turtle take data from each of the regions were being collected by headquarters. This official remarked that such data would be useful to him when making jeopardy determinations.

Similarly, FWS's national sea turtle coordinator told us that FWS recently developed a document in which the agency can collect data on all of the service's anticipated sea turtle take and that she plans to share this document with FWS field officials who conduct section 7 consultations on projects that may affect sea turtles. This step is encouraging, but we noted a number of limitations in the document that we believe could hinder its usefulness in calculating total anticipated take. For example, anticipated take is not expressed in a standardized format and instead may be expressed in terms of miles or square feet of affected beach. In one case an action was expected to affect 7.7 linear miles of beach, while in another the action was expected to affect almost 15,000 square feet. In addition, the document includes actions that may occur over different periods. For example, one action was expected to last 25 years, while another was expected to last only 8 months. This variability may also complicate any analysis of total anticipated take over a certain period.

In commenting on a draft of this report, Interior stated that FWS officials face difficulties in estimating and monitoring actual take. According to Interior, much of FWS's section 7 consultation involves beach nourishment projects. Most of the take associated with these projects is due to nests being destroyed because they were not detected and removed before construction activities began or due to a reduction in the number of new sea turtle nests established because of disturbance from construction activities. Such take would likely be small and difficult to detect, according to Interior's comments. Interior also commented that the reason FWS officials express take as the amount of beach area affected is the difficulty they face in estimating the actual number of sea turtles or nests that are likely to be destroyed. In addition, Interior stated that take is not expressed over a consistent time period because the agency is limited to analyzing take anticipated from proposed actions for the time periods that are requested, which may be for several months or over several years. According to Interior's comments, estimating, tracking, and analyzing take is further complicated by the fact that take may be lethal or nonlethal and may affect the turtles during different life stages. For example, because of the high natural mortality of sea turtles during their earlier life stages, take of sea turtle eggs and hatchlings caused by beach nourishment has much less reproductive impact on the population than take of older turtles in commercial fisheries under a NMFS take authorization.

Although we recognize the inherent difficulties involved in estimating and monitoring actual take, according to some experts and NMFS officials we spoke with, and previous work that we have conducted, it is important for the services to gather information on total take. Specifically, according to some experts and NMFS officials we spoke with, total take should be considered when making jeopardy determinations or approving additional take authorizations.[24] Such considerations are particularly important in the case of sea turtles because consultations occur at several NMFS regional and FWS regional and field offices, and sea turtles are both highly migratory and wide-ranging. Further, as we reported in May 2009, it is critical for federal staff involved in consultations to track total take for a species to strengthen their understanding of its status and to factor that knowledge into future consultation decisions.[25] We concluded at the time that without total take information for a species, FWS staff may not be able to effectively evaluate the collective impacts of federal actions over time, across multiple offices, and across species' ranges. Our report also noted that development of a systematic take-tracking system would be particularly useful for wide-ranging species. We recommended that FWS continue to develop existing databases, in as strategic and expeditious a manner as possible, to enable systematic tracking of cumulative take for all species affected by formal consultations.

Nevertheless, officials we spoke with from both services told us that because of limited funding, among other reasons, they have no plans to update any of the databases to require the entry of anticipated and actual take. For example, NMFS officials told us they plan to launch a new Public Consultation Tracking System in 2012, but because of a lack of funding, the new system is not likely to add a data field for actual take. In

---

[24]The services have been sued by environmental groups over the years because of how they calculate the environmental baseline for listed species. For example, one court held that an environmental baseline calculation was inadequate where the service merely listed the other activities affecting the species without making them part of its analysis. Defenders of Wildlife v. Babbitt, 130 F. Supp. 2d 121, 127-128 (D.D.C. 2001). When the agencies issued new biological opinions, the court clarified that a biological opinion is adequate if it takes the environmental baseline seriously and makes a concerted effort to evaluate the impact of the agency's proposed action against that backdrop. Defenders of Wildlife v. Norton, 2003 U.S. Dist. LEXIS 26558, (D.D.C. Jan. 7, 2003). In Oceana v. Evans, the same court specifically found that the environmental baseline analysis was adequate where it discussed anticipated take from other projects, even though it did not numerically add together take from different sources.

[25]GAO-09-550.

addition, according to an FWS official, no implementation schedule has been set for proposed enhancements to the Tracking and Integrated Logging System database. We believe that by not modifying their existing or planned databases, the services will not be able to use them to collect, analyze, or communicate complete information on anticipated and actual take that has been authorized. In commenting on a draft of this report, NOAA noted that NMFS is aware that some take occurs that has not been authorized by either NMFS or FWS, such as ongoing take in state fisheries, and that to have a comprehensive view of the status of sea turtle species requires consideration of both authorized and unauthorized take.

NMFS's and FWS's Biological Opinions Do Not Clearly Explain Rationales for Determining Whether an Action Will Jeopardize Sea Turtles

The services have jointly developed a handbook stating that a biological opinion stemming from a section 7 consultation under the Endangered Species Act should, among other things, be written so that the general public can understand the logic that led to the biological conclusion. But sea turtle experts told us, and we also found, that the services' biological opinions do not clearly describe how they reach their conclusions.[26] Some officials from both services acknowledged that their biological opinions are not always clear.

In 1998, NMFS and FWS jointly developed a handbook to provide internal guidance to assist staff responsible for preparing biological opinions as part of the section 7 consultation process. The handbook, among other things, emphasizes the importance of clarity and conciseness, stating that biological opinions should be written so the general public can understand the logic that led to the biological conclusion and be complete enough to withstand the rigors of a legal review.

---

[26]Our review focused solely on whether the biological opinions themselves were clear and transparent using the services' section 7 consultation handbook's criterion that the opinions should be written so the general public could understand the services' determinations. Our findings should not be interpreted as an assessment of whether the biological opinions adhere to applicable laws. Generally speaking, if the rationale of such an opinion were to be challenged in court, the court would apply a test that is fairly deferential to the service. It would not second-guess the service's scientific or technical decisions as long as a reasoned basis for the service's conclusions could reasonably be discerned from the entire administrative record supporting the opinion. See, for example, Oceana v. Evans, 384 F. Supp. 2d 203, 224-25. See also Alaska Dep't of Envtl. Conservation v. EPA, 540 U.S. 461, 497 (2004), and Bowman Transp., Inc. v. Arkansas-Best Freight Sys., Inc., 419 U.S. 281, 286 (1974).

Loggerhead *(Caretta caretta)*

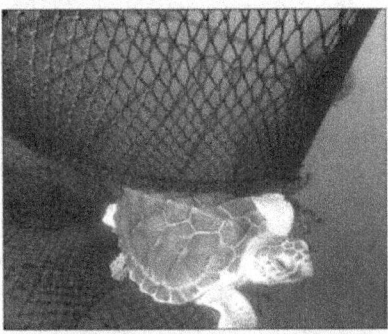

Source: National Oceanic and Atmospheric Administration.

Loggerheads are named after their large heads with powerful jaws, which enable them to feed on hard-shelled prey, such as whelks and conch. Adults average about 200 pounds in weight and may take about 35 years to reach sexual maturity. Highly migratory, they travel across both Atlantic and Pacific Oceans, as far north as Newfoundland and Alaska, and as far south as Argentina and Chile. Pacific loggerheads migrate more than 7,500 miles between nesting beaches in Japan and feeding grounds off Mexico; small juveniles drift among rafts of floating *Sargassum* seaweed. About 80 percent of loggerhead nesting in the southeastern United States occurs in six Florida counties. Females may lay more than 35 pounds of eggs during the approximately 3-month nesting season. The loggerhead was originally listed under the Endangered Species Act in 1978 as threatened, and in 2011 NMFS and FWS listed nine distinct population segments, four as threatened and five as endangered.

Despite the call for clarity in the services' handbook, some sea turtle experts we spoke with told us that they believe the opinions do not clearly explain how the services determined that an action anticipated to result in take of sea turtles will or will not jeopardize the species' continued existence. Furthermore, according to some experts and officials we spoke with, they believe the opinions also should make clear to what extent the service considered all sources of take. Without a full accounting of take previously authorized within a service and by the other service—as well as take resulting from other sources, such as fisheries not under federal jurisdiction—the opinions may not consider the full range of take that sea turtle populations are subjected to.

Our review of selected biological opinions developed by the services found a number of examples of these same concerns. Specifically, we found that:

- Although biological opinions can contain detailed information on, among other things, the proposed action, the species likely to be affected, and threats to their survival, it was not always clear how the services analyzed and synthesized the information presented into a determination of jeopardy or no jeopardy. For example:

  - In one NMFS biological opinion we reviewed, NMFS determined that over a 3-year period, despite a decline in the number of loggerhead nests on U.S. shores and a lack of data on the species' overall abundance, the anticipated lethal take of 346 loggerhead sea turtles by Atlantic shark fisheries would not measurably affect loggerhead survival. The biological opinion did not present a clear explanation of how NMFS reached this conclusion, however, and we could not trace the logic from the biological information presented in the opinion to the conclusion NMFS reached that this particular level of loggerhead sea turtle take would not jeopardize the species.

  - In one section 7 consultation about a proposed beach sand replenishment project, where some take of green, hawksbill, Kemp's ridley, leatherback, and loggerhead sea turtles was anticipated, the biological opinion prepared by FWS provided information about the species (such as population and nesting trends) and potential effects of the proposed action (such as burial of nests or hatchlings from the sand placement). But it was not clear from the opinion how such information was factored into the analysis or how FWS incorporated this information into the final jeopardy determination. This biological opinion was particularly confusing because the conclusion discusses the take in terms of the number of miles of beach affected, not the number of nests affected, as one would have expected from the information presented in the body of the opinion.

- The opinions do not always make clear the extent to which all sources of take for a species were considered. For example:

  - In a biological opinion we reviewed concerning the spiny dogfish fishery, NMFS describes 12 other fisheries operating in the same geographic area for which it had previously authorized the take of loggerhead, leatherback, Kemp's ridley, and green turtles. Although NMFS's biological opinion for the spiny dogfish fishery acknowledged the existence of the 12 other fisheries, the text of the opinion did not state the extent to which NMFS considered the cumulative take of all 13 fisheries in determining whether the spiny dogfish fishery would jeopardize the four sea turtle species in that area.

  - Three biological opinions prepared by FWS within one 6-month period focused on the effects on the green, hawksbill, Kemp's ridley, leatherback, and loggerhead sea turtles of replenishing beaches in three "action areas" within a single Florida county. In each of the three opinions, FWS concluded that the relatively small percentage of beach affected by the proposed action would not jeopardize the species. What is not clear from our review of the biological opinions, however, is whether or to what extent FWS considered, among other factors, the anticipated take from the first of the three projects when developing the second opinion or considered the anticipated take from the first two projects when developing the third opinion. Under the Endangered Species Act, the environmental baseline section of the services' biological opinions must consider the anticipated impacts of other activities that have undergone or are undergoing section 7 consultation in the action area. At least one court has noted, however, that the services must consider all information about threats both within and outside the action area in making jeopardy determinations.[27]

Some officials from both services acknowledged that the biological opinions they prepare are not always clear. Specifically, some NMFS officials we spoke with acknowledged that their opinions are not always transparent. In fact, materials used to train NMFS staff on how to write effective biological opinions have also recognized this weakness. Specifically, the training materials note that biological opinions routinely do not link the facts and evidence to conclusions and, as a result, "leave readers to form a picture of how this evidence supports our conclusion." FWS officials also told us that including clear and transparent rationales in biological opinions is a struggle for all listed species, not just sea turtles. Nonetheless, if the analyses and decisions documented in biological opinions are not transparent, neither Congress nor the public can be assured that the services are adequately protecting vulnerable sea turtle populations as required by the Endangered Species Act.

Neither NMFS nor FWS Has Developed Its Own Operational Plan on How to Achieve the Goals Established in Sea Turtle Recovery Plans

Neither service has developed its own operational plan describing the actions it will take to achieve goals set forth by sea turtle recovery plans. In the absence of such service-specific operational plans, officials we spoke with from each service said they use the recovery plans to guide their sea turtle protection activities. We found, however, that these recovery plans do not include key elements of effective planning, that the services do not always consider the recovery plans' goals when performing day-to-day activities, and that the jointly developed recovery plans do not provide each service with operational plans specific to each service. As a result, some regional NMFS officials are beginning to develop such plans, although FWS officials are not.

The services have developed 11 joint sea turtle recovery plans, which provide guidance that includes both high-level goals and specific actions that the services use to guide their recovery efforts. We did not review

---

[27]The court noted that the Endangered Species Act's regulations allow FWS to limit its cumulative effects analysis to the action area for the project being examined, but the service's evaluation of the species' current status and ultimate jeopardy determination are not limited in geographic scope. Rock Creek Alliance v. United States Fish & Wildlife Service, 390 F. Supp. 2d 993, 1001, 1010 (D. Mont. 2005). Thus, FWS must examine the current status of a species across its entire range, along with the effects of the action in the action area, to make a jeopardy determination.

these plans for compliance with the legal requirements for such plans under the Endangered Species Act. Instead, we reviewed them to see whether they included key elements of effective planning, which we have identified in previous work.[28] Our review found that they do not. For example, our prior work on strategic planning has shown that an effective plan should describe, among other things, specific activities managers and staff are to engage in to meet the plan's goals, as well as how an agency's performance goals relate to the plan's overall goals. But we found that the joint sea turtle recovery plans provide both services with high-level goals and some specific actions and direction for recovery efforts without detailing specific activities each service's managers and staff are to engage in to achieve these goals and without linking the services' annual performance goals to recovery plan goals. For example, the Northwest Atlantic loggerhead recovery plan sets a goal of increasing nests annually to at least 14,000 in certain areas. The recovery plan describes high-level actions (such as establishing a network of study sites to monitor trends in the species' abundance while at sea), but it does not lay out specific steps the services should take or the performance measures they should use to ensure they are making progress toward achieving this goal.

Moreover, some experts and NMFS officials indicated that the services have not always considered the goals laid out in recovery plans when performing day-to-day activities related to sea turtles or when writing biological opinions and making jeopardy determinations that authorize take. Specifically, one researcher commented that the services have "an incredible tool" in the form of species recovery plans but that there is a "disconnect" between these plans and the biological opinions they prepare. Specifically, in the view of individuals knowledgeable about sea turtles, biological opinions should, but currently do not, demonstrate how take anticipated from a proposed action will not hinder progress toward recovery plan goals. Similarly, some experts and officials from NMFS science centers observed that biological opinions make little reference to recovery plans and that it is difficult to understand how the criteria for recovery laid out in these plans factor in when NMFS determines in an opinion whether a proposed action will jeopardize sea turtle populations. In commenting on a draft of this report, Interior stated that FWS has

---

[28]GAO, *Agencies' Strategic Plans under GPRA: Key Questions to Facilitate Congressional Review*, GAO/GGD-10.1.16 (Washington, D.C.: May 1997).

Olive ridley *(Lepidochelys olivacea)*

Source: © 2003 Michael P. Jensen.

Olive ridleys are small—reaching 2 to 2.5 feet in length and a weight of 80 to 110 pounds. On reaching sexual maturity after about 15 years, females nest in enormous *arribadas*: one *arribada* in India was estimated to consist of 200,000 turtles nesting at the same time. Nesting occurs in nearly 40 countries worldwide. Although olive ridleys are regarded as the most abundant sea turtle species, they may also be the most exploited, as killing of adults takes place on nesting beaches and animals become entangled in fishing gear. According to the International Union for Conservation of Nature, the population has declined by about 50 percent since the 1960s; even with recent increases in some nesting populations, the overall reduction is greater than the overall increase. Olive ridleys were originally listed under the Endangered Species Act in 1978. Breeding populations on the Pacific coast of Mexico are listed as endangered, and all other populations are listed as threatened.

mentioned recovery goals in the service's biological opinions for the last 2 to 3 years.

In addition, jointly developed recovery plans do not provide each service with operational plans specific to each service. NMFS and FWS officials told us that the services rely on the recovery plans to help set priorities for each sea turtle species and to obtain funding for actions in line with these priorities. For example, NMFS officials told us that the service's Southwest Fisheries Science Center established a marine turtle program in 1998 in response to a recovery plan for sea turtles in the Pacific. The recovery plans, however, apply to the collective sea turtle protection efforts of both NMFS and FWS and consequently do not provide each service with its own operational blueprint for working toward the recovery plans' goals. For example, all the plans include cost estimates associated with recovery actions, but because the plans cover both services, they do not provide each service with an estimate of the resources it will need to achieve recovery goals. We believe that service-specific operational plans could describe the specific tasks to be completed on an annual basis by managers and staff for each individual service to implement the recovery actions identified in the recovery plans. Although there is no legal requirement to prepare them, without such plans and performance measures specific to NMFS and FWS, managers from each service, Congress, and the public cannot be assured that the services are each taking, and being held accountable for, the steps needed to achieve the goals articulated in sea turtle recovery plans.

Recognizing the lack of a national NMFS-specific sea turtle operational plan, NMFS officials from one region we spoke with said they are developing an operational plan for their region, and two other regions have already developed such plans for their regions. For example, officials from one region told us they are developing a region-specific plan because they believe that a regional plan is needed to identify region-specific activities, such as establishing milestones to gauge their progress toward meeting the recovery goals. The two NMFS region-specific plans we reviewed contain elements of effective plans, such as results-oriented goals. The plans also include elements that are absent from sea turtle recovery plans, such as links between those activities and specific steps managers and staff are to take and strategies to hold managers accountable. NMFS's northeastern regional office, for example, developed a 5-year plan that identifies the region's direction and goals. The plan includes a schedule to implement its sea turtle recovery efforts for fiscal year 2011. The schedule outlines the sea turtle program's goals and activities needed to achieve them, a plan for accomplishing the activities, an anticipated completion date for the activities, a specific staff person responsible for each activity, the funding required to complete an activity, and the status of the activity. Such region-specific operational plans, however, do not exist for all of NMFS's regional offices.

FWS officials, on the other hand, told us that their regional and field offices have not developed FWS-specific sea turtle operational plans and do not believe such plans are needed. The officials explained that because the vast majority of sea turtle nesting occurs in Region 4 where the national sea turtle coordinator is located, they did not believe that developing formal operational plans was necessary. Further, officials told us that because the service itself cannot directly implement recovery plan goals, they do not believe they need a service-specific plan for achieving them. For example, service officials told us that they work with conservation partners such as the states and nongovernmental organizations to put recovery measures in place—such as revisions of local ordinances to minimize the impact of beach lighting on sea turtle hatchlings. Nevertheless, an operational plan would allow the service to identify steps, such as conducting outreach and education, developing model ordinances, or establishing grant programs, that could direct and better facilitate the conservation partners' actions toward the recovery plan goals.

Conclusions

For wide-ranging species like sea turtles, which spend some time both on land and in the sea, coordination between federal agencies tasked with their protection is vital. NMFS and FWS have coordinated on some sea turtle protection activities, such as developing recovery plans, but the services do not consistently coordinate before issuing an incidental take statement under section 7 of the Endangered Species Act. A memorandum of understanding broadly defines some of the services' coordination responsibilities under the act, but it is silent on whether the services should share take data related to section 7 of the act, which constitutes the majority of take. It also does not clearly articulate the coordination-related steps each service is to take before issuing or denying a take permit or specify how the services are to share take data. Without knowing the extent of take anticipated by the counterpart service, each service is missing information about the status of sea turtle species, information that could assist in preparing biological opinions. Effective coordination is made more difficult by the fact that the services do not comprehensively require entry of anticipated and actual take information in the databases they use to manage section 7 consultations and section

10 permits. Compiling and analyzing data on anticipated and actual take could help officials determine how many turtles the services have authorized be removed from existing populations and would give them another tool that could help gauge the success of their sea turtle protection efforts.

Furthermore, the biological opinions NMFS and FWS develop in association with section 7 consultations do not clearly explain the analyses and rationales used in determining whether proposed actions will jeopardize sea turtles. Without a clear explanation of the analyses and key factors leading to each determination of jeopardy or no jeopardy, the general public cannot easily trace the services' logic and be assured that the anticipated level of take will not jeopardize sea turtles. Finally, the services do not have service-specific operational plans to help them achieve the goals of the jointly developed sea turtle recovery plans. Without operational plans that include key elements—such as specific activities, milestones, and performance measures—and that each service coordinates among the regional and field offices and with the other service, neither NMFS or FWS can assure Congress or the public that it is making progress in protecting sea turtle populations.

Recommendations for Executive Action

To improve the effectiveness of the services' sea turtle protection and recovery efforts, we recommend that the Secretary of Commerce direct the National Oceanic and Atmospheric Administration's Assistant Administrator for Fisheries, and that the Secretary of the Interior direct the Director of FWS, to take the following four actions:

1. Revise the existing memorandum of understanding to clarify what specific steps the services will take to coordinate before issuing or denying sea turtle take permits, steps that, at a minimum, should include sharing data on the take each service has authorized. In addition, the memorandum should be revised to include section 7 take statements, and the services should adhere to the terms of the revised memorandum.

2. Modify each service's existing databases or develop new ones to require entry and analysis of authorized and actual take data.

3. Direct NMFS and FWS staff to write biological opinions so that the analyses they conduct and the rationale they use in arriving at the

jeopardy or no jeopardy determination for actions anticipated to result in the take of sea turtles are clearer and more transparent.

4. Develop operational plans specific to NMFS and FWS, which should describe the activities each service will perform to achieve the goals established in sea turtle recovery plans and include key elements of effective plans that we identified in this report. Such plans should be coordinated among the regional and field offices within both services, as well as between the services' headquarters.

Agency Comments and Our Evaluation

We provided a draft of this report to the Departments of Commerce and the Interior for comment. In its written comments, reproduced in appendix II, NOAA, providing comments on behalf of Commerce, generally agreed with our recommendations. In commenting on the recommendation that the services update the memorandum of understanding, NOAA agreed and stated that it will work with FWS to determine whether modifications or additions are necessary. In response to the recommendation that the services modify their databases or develop new ones, NOAA agreed that improvements to the existing databases would consolidate take information in a streamlined manner, but it noted that such modifications are contingent on reprioritization of existing or additional resources for such changes. NOAA also said that it often faced significant challenges gathering information on some of the largest sources of in-water takes, such as take from fisheries.

In response to the recommendation that the services more clearly explain in biological opinions the rationale for their jeopardy determinations, NOAA said that while it believes that its biological opinions meet all legal standards of the Endangered Species Act and the Administrative Procedure Act, it recognizes the benefit of ensuring that biological opinions contain an explanation sufficient to ensure that the basis of the opinion is understandable and transparent to members of the general public who may not read the full administrative record that would be provided to a court. NOAA also said that it will review its quality assurance and training mechanisms to determine whether additional actions are needed to improve the clarity of biological opinions. NOAA suggested a rewording of the recommendation, and we have modified the recommendation to clarify it. In response to our final recommendation— that each service develop operational plans to help achieve the goals in sea turtle recovery plans—NOAA stated that implementation of recovery plans depends on availability of funds and that it would work internally, as well as externally with FWS, to determine whether additional planning activities would enhance the recovery and conservation of listed sea turtles.

In addition, NOAA included some general comments on the draft report. In particular, NOAA stated that by not recognizing the lack of data and information for many fundamental aspects of both sea turtle biology and ecology, and the effects of human-caused activities on sea turtles, the draft report was missing an important contextual element. NOAA stated that these data gaps are important to consider when assessing the performance of any recovery and conservation program. We acknowledge that such data gaps exist, but we believe that in light of these gaps, improved coordination, data collection, and planning are especially important to assist the services with their sea turtle protection efforts. NOAA also raised a concern about our finding that biological opinions should provide more clarity for the general public, and NOAA stated that all of its opinions provide an appropriate explanation for its jeopardy or no jeopardy determination. NOAA also recommended that we clarify that our report did not attempt to review the opinions as a court would, with the benefit of an agency's full administrative record. We did not review the services' biological opinions to assess the legal sufficiency of the analyses or jeopardy determinations contained in the biological opinions. Rather, we reviewed selected sea turtle biological opinions for clarity and transparency, as called for in the services' joint consultation handbook. We added some additional language to the report to further reinforce these points. Finally, NOAA stated that it disagrees that compilation and analysis of anticipated and actual take are requirements for consultation or gauging the adequacy of sea turtle protection and recovery measures. Our report does not state that collection and analysis of such data are or should be required. Instead our report explains that on the basis of previous GAO work and according to some experts and officials we spoke with, it is important for the services to gather information on total take to help inform their sea turtle conservation decisions. NOAA said it believed some confusion and inaccuracies existed in the report's background section and suggested some technical changes. While we believe the information presented in this section of the report is clear and accurate, we have considered NOAA's comments and have made changes as appropriate. NOAA also provided other technical comments that we incorporated as appropriate.

In its written comments, reproduced in appendix III, Interior generally concurred with our recommendations and also provided some general comments. In particular, Interior said that the report did not adequately acknowledge the difficulty of determining and analyzing take of sea turtles. We have added such a discussion to the report. Nevertheless, while we acknowledge the difficulty of determining and analyzing actual take data, we continue to believe that if the services do not track the actual effects of the take they authorize, they will lack a useful tool for helping ensure that their actions are protecting sea turtles. In addition, Interior stated that the report appears to criticize FWS for describing anticipated take of sea turtles in its section 7 consultations as beach miles affected rather than the number of sea turtles or nests that would be destroyed. Interior stated that the report fails to acknowledge that such descriptions are used because of the difficulty in estimating actual numbers of individuals or nests taken. We do not believe that our report criticizes the use of habitat descriptions, such as beach miles, and in fact the report includes information stating that their use is legally permissible. We continue to believe, however, that the services should comprehensively collect and analyze take data and that not reporting these data in a consistent format complicates analysis. Interior also provided technical comments that we incorporated as appropriate.

As agreed with your offices, unless you publicly announce the contents of this report earlier, we plan no further distribution until 30 days from the report date. At that time, we will send copies to the Secretaries of Commerce and the Interior, the appropriate congressional committees, and other interested parties. In addition, the report will be available at no charge on the GAO website at http://www.gao.gov.

If you or your staff have any questions about this report, please contact me at (202) 512-3841 or mittala@gao.gov. Contact points for our Offices of Congressional Relations and Public Affairs may be found on the last page of this report. GAO staff who made key contributions to this report are listed in appendix IV.

Anu K. Mittal
Director, Natural Resources and Environment

Appendix I: Objectives, Scope, and Methodology

The objectives for this review were to examine the extent to which the National Marine Fisheries Service (NMFS) and the Fish and Wildlife Service (FWS) (1) coordinate their sea turtle protection activities, (2) collect and analyze data on anticipated and actual sea turtle take, (3) clearly explain in their biological opinions the rationales they use when determining whether a proposed action will jeopardize sea turtles, and (4) have developed operational plans to help realize the goals of recovery plans for sea turtle species.

We addressed these objectives by taking a variety of steps. To gain a national perspective on the services' (NMFS and FWS) sea turtle protection efforts, we reviewed relevant federal laws and regulations, such as the Endangered Species Act, as well as relevant agency documentation, such as the services' joint guidance for the act's section 7 consultations. We reviewed studies and other documents on sea turtle protection issues, including peer-reviewed scientific journals, government-sponsored research, and reports from nongovernmental organizations. We also reviewed relevant prior GAO reports. In addition, we interviewed NMFS's and FWS's national sea turtle coordinators and officials with national sea turtle protection responsibilities. We also interviewed a range of experts and other individuals—including university researchers; representatives of nongovernmental organizations, such as Oceana; and representatives from regional fishery management councils[1]—whom we identified as knowledgeable about national sea turtle protection efforts. We used the following categories to quantify responses of experts, officials, and other individuals knowledgeable about sea turtles: "some" refers to 2 to 5 respondents, "several" refers to 6 to 10 respondents, and "many" refers to 11 or more respondents. We obtained sea turtle information used in the sidebars from NMFS and FWS.

To examine the services' sea turtle protection efforts in greater depth, and to better understand any regional differences, we selected a nonprobability sample of four states—Florida, Hawaii, Massachusetts, and Texas. We selected these states primarily on the basis of the existence of sea turtle nesting populations in the state, federal fisheries

---

[1]Regional fishery management councils are composed of federal and state fishery management officials as well as active participants in the fishery, among others, and are respons ble for developing management plans for fisheries in federal waters.

offshore,[2] and a relatively high level of anticipated take associated with commercial fishing operations. For our selected locations, we analyzed documentation from and conducted interviews with a diverse range of individuals involved in sea turtle protection, including the services' regional and field office officials; other federal and state agency officials; and experts from industry, such as the Southern Shrimp Alliance, and from environmental groups, such as the Sea Turtle Conservancy.

In addition to the steps outlined above, which were common to all the objectives, we also took other steps specific to a particular objective. To determine the extent to which the services coordinate their sea turtle protection activities, we reviewed the memorandum of understanding between NMFS and FWS concerning their sea turtle protection activities. To assess the extent to which the services collect and analyze data on anticipated and actual sea turtle take, we reviewed information about the following databases: NMFS's Public Consultation Tracking System, NMFS's Authorizations and Permits for Protected Species, FWS's Tracking and Integrated Logging System, and FWS's Service Permit Issuance and Tracking System.

To determine the extent to which the services clearly explain in their biological opinions the rationale they use when making decisions about how much sea turtle take is anticipated to result from reviewed actions, we analyzed NMFS and FWS biological opinions for anticipated sea turtle take under section 7 of the act. NMFS's Public Consultation Tracking System and FWS's Tracking and Integrated Logging System databases contain a record of section 7 formal consultations for which biological opinions have been prepared. To assess the reliability of these databases, we conducted electronic testing for missing data and obvious errors and interviewed relevant officials. We found the data from the databases to be sufficiently reliable for the purpose of identifying the universe of biological opinions prepared by NMFS and FWS. Specifically, we reviewed all 22 of the biological opinions issued from January 1, 2006, to January 1, 2011, by NMFS for federal fisheries. Using data from the Tracking and Integrated Logging System database, we determined that FWS conducted 119 formal section 7 consultations within our time frame

---

[2]The term "fishery" means one or more stocks of fish which can be treated as a unit for purposes of conservation and management and which are identified on the basis of geographical, scientific, technical, recreational, and economic characteristics. We use the term "federal fishery" to mean a fishery managed by the regional councils and NMFS.

that anticipated sea turtle take. We selected a random sample of 30, which allowed us to review a wide range of biological opinions but does not allow us to generalize to the entire population of 119 opinions. Subsequently, 9 FWS opinions from the random sample of 30 were determined to be outside the scope of our review and were not included in the analysis for the following reasons: (1) FWS incorrectly categorized the consultation as a formal consultation when it was an informal consultation, (2) the biological opinion is still in draft form, and (3) the biological opinion did not involve anticipated take of sea turtles.

We reviewed each biological opinion to determine whether the services clearly and transparently explained the rationale for the jeopardy determination. We considered a biological opinion to be clear and transparent if we determined that there was a direct link to or explanation of (1) how information included in the opinion, such as nesting trends or population data, was factored into the jeopardy determination or (2) how all other sources of take were factored into the jeopardy determination. One analyst conducted the initial review. Particular emphasis was placed on the review of the following sections in the opinions (although names used vary between the services): "Status of the Species," "Environmental Baseline," "Effects of the Action," and "Jeopardy Determination/Conclusion." After the initial review, a second GAO analyst then reviewed those biological opinions that one analyst determined were not clear and transparent to verify that we had correctly categorized the opinions and to identify any conflicting findings, which were discussed and resolved between the two analysts.

To evaluate the extent to which NMFS and FWS have developed operational plans to help achieve the goals of recovery plans for sea turtles, we reviewed all the sea turtle recovery plans and other related plans developed by the services to guide their sea turtle protection activities. Specifically, we reviewed all 11 sea turtle recovery plans and 2 regional sea turtle plans to determine the extent to which they contained elements of effective planning as contained in GAO guidance on the Government Performance and Results Act.[3] One analyst conducted the initial review. Particular emphasis was placed on review of the "Recovery Narrative" and "Implementation Schedule" sections of the recovery plans.

---

[3]GAO, *Agencies' Strategic Plans under GPRA: Key Questions to Facilitate Congressional Review*, GAO/GGD-10.1.16 (Washington, D.C.: May 1997).

After the initial review, a second GAO analyst then reviewed each plan to
verify that it had been characterized correctly or to identify any conflicting
findings, which were discussed and resolved between the two reviewers.

We conducted this performance audit from February 2011 to January
2012, in accordance with generally accepted government auditing
standards. Those standards require that we plan and perform the audit to
obtain sufficient, appropriate evidence to provide a reasonable basis for
our findings and conclusions based on our audit objectives. We believe
that the evidence obtained provides a reasonable basis for our findings
and conclusions based on our audit objectives.

Appendix II: Comments from the Department of Commerce

UNITED STATES DEPARTMENT OF COMMERCE
The Under Secretary of Commerce
for Oceans and Atmosphere
Washington, D.C. 20230

JAN 18 2012

Anu K. Mittal
Director
Natural Resources and Environment
U.S. Government Accountability Office
441 G Street, NW
Washington, DC 20548

Dear Ms. Mittal:

Thank you for the opportunity to review and comment on the Government Accountability Office's draft report entitled *Endangered Sea Turtles: Better Coordination, Data Collection, and Planning Could Improve Federal Protection and Recovery Efforts* (GAO-12-242). On behalf of the Department of Commerce, I enclose the National Oceanic and Atmospheric Administration's programmatic comments to the draft report.

Sincerely,

Dr. Jane Lubchenco
Under Secretary of Commerce
for Oceans and Atmosphere

Enclosure

THE ADMINISTRATOR

Department of Commerce
National Oceanic and Atmospheric Administration
Comments to the Draft GAO Report Entitled
"Endangered Sea Turtles, Better Coordination, and Planning
Could Improve Federal Protection and Recovery Efforts"
(GAO-12-242, January 2012)

<u>**General Comments**</u>

The National Oceanic and Atmospheric Administration (NOAA) appreciates the opportunity to respond to the Government Accountability Office (GAO) report on coordination and planning to improve federal sea turtle protection and recovery efforts. The report primarily focuses on NOAA's and the Department of Interior, U.S. Fish and Wildlife Service's data management and use of incidental and directed take information. The report's discussion of how NOAA assembles and uses these data could more accurately reflect current efforts. In addition to addressing NOAA's specific comments, we urge GAO to again review our previously submitted comments on the Statement of Facts to ensure that the included information and discussions are clear, factual, and unambiguous.

A key aspect and important contextual element missing in the report is recognition of the lack of data and information for many fundamental aspects of both sea turtle biology/ecology and the effects of anthropogenic activities on sea turtles. This was discussed with GAO analysts during the review period. Sea turtles present especially difficult challenges as the species are wide-ranging, highly migratory, and there are multiple life stages each with diverse life history strategies (and large knowledge gaps remain to varying degrees for each life stage). Our data on anthropogenic effects is also limited due to the difficulties of assessing effects on the high seas, in remote areas, and on poorly understood life stages. These data gaps are important to consider, and at least describe, when assessing the performance of any recovery and conservation program. One of the best ways to understand and track turtle populations is to implement a robust population monitoring program.

NOAA remains concerned about the impact of GAO stating that biological opinions, including identified opinions, do not clearly explain the rationale for the determination that an action is or is not likely to jeopardize sea turtles. NOAA believes that all of its biological opinions provide appropriate explanation for the jeopardy/no jeopardy determination. NOAA is concerned that the discussion in this report could be viewed as the GAO opining as to whether the opinions meet legal standards. NOAA recommends changes, **Recommended Changes in Discussion of Biological Opinions,** to clarify that GAO is not attempting to review the opinions as a court would - with the benefit of an agency's full administrative record and based on applicable standards of review - but rather is seeking to assure that the basis of the opinions is understandable and transparent for the public who may not review the entire record.

NOAA disagrees that compilation and analysis of actual and anticipated take is a requirement for consultation or for gauging whether sea turtle protection and recovery measures are adequate. NOAA is concerned that GAO statements to this effect could be interpreted as suggesting the requirement that the Services must make a collective finding of jeopardy based on the take resulting from all federal actions. This position has been rejected. See e.g. *Oceana v. Evans,*

1

384 F.Supp.2d 203, 230 (D.D.C. 2005), citing *Defenders of Wildlife v. Norton, 2003 WL 24122459 (D.D.C. Jan. 7, 2003)* at 5. NOAA also notes that its biologists are well aware of all sources of take of sea turtles and consider all sources of take in its biological opinions. NOAA suggests some changes in **Recommended Changes in Discussion of Biological Opinions** to clarify this point.

NOAA also continues to note some confusion and inaccuracies in the Background section of this report, and therefore proposes suggested changes for this section. All of our proposed changes appear after our response to GAO's specific recommendations.

NOAA Response to GAO Recommendations

The draft GAO report states, "To improve the effectiveness of the Services' sea turtle protection and recovery efforts, we recommend that the Secretary of Commerce direct the National Oceanic and Atmospheric Administration's Assistant Administrator for Fisheries, and that the Secretary of the Interior direct the Director of FWS, to take the following four actions:"

Recommendation 1: "Revise the existing memorandum of understanding to clarify what specific steps the Services will take to coordinate before issuing or denying sea turtle take permits, steps that, at a minimum, should include sharing data on the take each Service has authorized. In addition, the memorandum should be revised to include section 7 take statements, and the Services should adhere to the terms of the revised memorandum."

NOAA Response: NOAA agrees that the Services should jointly review the Memorandum of Understanding (MOU) signed by the Services in 1977. NOAA will work with the U.S. Fish and Wildlife Service (USFWS) to determine whether any modifications or additions to the MOU, including coordination regarding Endangered Species Act (ESA) Section 7 and Section 10, are necessary to enhance sea turtle recovery and conservation.

Recommendation 2: "Modify each Service's existing databases or develop new ones to require entry and analysis of authorized and actual take data."

NOAA Response: NOAA agrees that improvements to the existing databases would consolidate known take information in a more streamlined manner. However, NOAA notes that modifications/improvements to existing databases are contingent on the reprioritization of existing or additional resources to carry out such changes.

Additionally, our ability to estimate takes and to quantify actual takes is limited. While we can track individual takes for smaller projects with better precision, we often face significant challenges gathering information on some of the largest sources of in-water takes: fishery bycatch. Limited observer coverage in some fisheries results in uncertainty in the calculation of actual take levels. For other fisheries, such as the Hawaii longline fishery, we have very precise knowledge of actual take levels. The nature of the fishery, the type of bycatch reduction measures that may be required, and the magnitude of the fishery all bear on the feasibility and effectiveness of observer programs.

Additionally, we lack robust take levels for many, if not most, state waters fisheries and international fisheries. Dedicating limited resources to improving, establishing, and maintaining

2

databases could take away resources that may allow us to gather and/or improve the information necessary to populate such databases in a meaningful way.

With regard to the Authorizations and Permits for Protected Species (APPS) database for 10(a)(1)(A) scientific research permits, as noted in the report, the entry of authorized take information into APPS is already required. Entry of actual take information into APPS would require staffing resources that are not available at this time. Also noted in the report, the analysis of take data is currently accomplished by permit analysts using a suite of resources, including the APPS database. Developing queries in APPS that would allow for the analysis of authorized and actual takes solely using APPS is dependent on funding for database programming.

With regard to NOAA's Public Consultation Tracking System (PCTS), this system would need to be upgraded to expand and require certain fields. Revisions to the system are contingent on reprioritization of funding and resources.

We also stress that any analysis of the anticipated take in biological opinions would require individual examination of each opinion to understand how the extent and amount of take was derived. For some federal actions, we can only estimate an extent of take based on a geographic area or the frequency of event of exposure (e.g., seismic surveys where we cannot know how many sea turtles are exposed). In these cases, we may combine sea turtle species in one take number where multiple species may be exposed to the activity. Additionally, all known take of sea turtles, including take not authorized under Section 7, is considered during the Section 7 consultation process.

Recommendation 3: "Direct NMFS and FWS staff to more clearly explain and document in biological opinions the analyses they conducted and the rationale they used in arriving at the final jeopardy determination for actions anticipated to result in the take of sea turtles."

NOAA Response: NOAA suggests rewording Recommendation 3 to read:

"Direct NMFS and FWS staff to write biological opinions so that the analyses they conducted and the rationale they used to arrive at the jeopardy/no jeopardy determination are understandable to members of the general public."

In their joint Endangered Species Consultation Handbook, the Services have provided guidance that biological opinions should be written so that the general public could trace the logic of the opinion and complete enough to withstand judicial review. NOAA believes that its biological opinions meet all legal standards of the Endangered Species Act and the Administrative Procedure Act. However, NOAA recognizes the benefit of ensuring that biological opinions contain an explanation that is sufficient to assure that the basis of the opinion is understandable and transparent to members of the public who may not read the full administrative record that would be provided to a court. NOAA will review the quality assurance and training mechanisms in place pursuant to its policy directive for delegation of authority for section 7 consultations under the ESA (NMFS Policy Directive 02-110-12) to determine whether additional actions are necessary to improve the clarity of biological opinions to ensure that the rationale used is clear and understandable to a general reader. In some cases, the perceived lack of clarity in Section 7 consultations may result from the lack of robust population data on some species and/or life stages of listed sea turtles. This is an ongoing challenge.

3

Recommendation 4: "Develop operational plans specific to NMFS and FWS, which should describe the activities each Service will perform to achieve the goals established in sea turtle recovery plans and include key elements of effective plans that we identified in this report. Such plans should be coordinated among the regional and field offices within both Services, as well as between the Services' headquarters."

NOAA Response: NOAA believes that the federal Recovery Plans for sea turtles, concluded in accordance with Section 4 of the ESA, provide the blueprint for recovery of these species. The Implementation Schedules, included with each Recovery Plan, lay out the specific actions and priorities, responsible parties, and estimated costs. Implementation of recovery actions is dependent on availability of funds. NOAA will work internally as well as externally with USFWS to determine whether additional planning activities would enhance recovery and conservation of listed sea turtles.

4

Appendix III: Comments from the Department of the Interior

United States Department of the Interior

OFFICE OF THE SECRETARY
Washington, DC 20240

JAN 12 2012

Ms. Anu K. Mittal
Director
Natural Resources and Environment
Government Accountability Office
Washington, D.C. 20548

Dear Ms. Mittal:

The Department of the Interior (Department) appreciates GAO's review of coordination, data collection, and planning related to listed sea turtles. Thank you for giving the Department the opportunity to review and comment on the GAO draft report entitled, *ENDANGERED SEA TURTLES: Better Coordination, Data Collection, and Planning Could Improve Federal Protection and Recovery Efforts,* (GAO-12-242).

The Department generally concurs with the recommendations. The enclosure contains general and technical comments for your consideration.

If you have any questions about this response please contact Kathy Garrity at (703)358-2551.

Sincerely,

Rachel Jacobson
Acting Assistant Secretary for Fish and Wildlife and Parks

Enclosure

DOI Comments on the GAO Draft Report
ENDANGERED SEA TURTLES:
Better Coordination, Data Collection, and Planning Could Improve Federal Protection and
Recovery Efforts (GAO-12-242)

General Comments

Here are some general comments regarding section 7 consultations:

The report has not incorporated any of the previous discussions on the inherent difficulty of
determining "actual take" for sea turtles. Much of the U.S. Fish and Wildlife Service's (FWS)
section 7 consultation involves beach nourishment projects. Our requirements include prior
beach monitoring to determine the location and number of sea turtle nests in the nourishment
area. Prior to construction activities, the nests that would be smothered by sand placement or
crushed beneath construction equipment are relocated away from the activities so they are spared
from direct take. Although there is some likely reduction in hatching success, most of the take
anticipated would be for nests not detected by beach monitoring prior to construction or
reduction of sea turtle nesting effort as a result of construction related disturbance. Such
parameters would represent small and difficult to detect take levels that could not be monitored.
For in-water activities, finding an accurate measure of take associated with a given project or
program would also be difficult since bodies recovered from a large expanse of water would be
few and far between, and presumably a fraction of the actual deaths. By not acknowledging this
difficulty, recommendations in the report represent overly simplified solutions to complex and
difficult issues.

Similarly, the report appears to criticize the FWS for anticipating take during section 7
consultations as beach miles or beach area instead of the number of individuals or nests that
would be destroyed. As indicated above, the report fails to acknowledge that the reason these
indices are used in the first place is based on the difficulty of estimating actual numbers of
individuals or sea turtle nests taken. Given a lack of ability to detect or monitor this take in
terms of individuals or nests destroyed, making such an estimate of take may not be a useful
exercise. Again, without an acknowledgement in the report of this difficulty, the
recommendations represent overly simplified solutions that are impractical to implement.

1

Appendix IV: GAO Contact and Staff Acknowledgments

GAO Contact	Anu K. Mittal, (202) 512-3841 or mittala@gao.gov
Staff Acknowledgments	In addition to the contact named above, Stephen D. Secrist (Assistant Director), Jenna Beveridge, Antoinette Capaccio, Ellen W. Chu, Justin Fisher, Griffin Glatt, Marietta Revesz, Rebecca Shea, and Lisa Vojta made key contributions to this report.

GAO's Mission	The Government Accountability Office, the audit, evaluation, and investigative arm of Congress, exists to support Congress in meeting its constitutional responsibilities and to help improve the performance and accountability of the federal government for the American people. GAO examines the use of public funds; evaluates federal programs and policies; and provides analyses, recommendations, and other assistance to help Congress make informed oversight, policy, and funding decisions. GAO's commitment to good government is reflected in its core values of accountability, integrity, and reliability.
Obtaining Copies of GAO Reports and Testimony	The fastest and easiest way to obtain copies of GAO documents at no cost is through GAO's website (www.gao.gov). Each weekday afternoon, GAO posts on its website newly released reports, testimony, and correspondence. To have GAO e-mail you a list of newly posted products, go to www.gao.gov and select "E-mail Updates."
Order by Phone	The price of each GAO publication reflects GAO's actual cost of production and distribution and depends on the number of pages in the publication and whether the publication is printed in color or black and white. Pricing and ordering information is posted on GAO's website, http://www.gao.gov/ordering.htm. Place orders by calling (202) 512-6000, toll free (866) 801-7077, or TDD (202) 512-2537. Orders may be paid for using American Express, Discover Card, MasterCard, Visa, check, or money order. Call for additional information.
Connect with GAO	Connect with GAO on Facebook, Flickr, Twitter, and YouTube. Subscribe to our RSS Feeds or E-mail Updates. Listen to our Podcasts. Visit GAO on the web at www.gao.gov.
To Report Fraud, Waste, and Abuse in Federal Programs	Contact: Website: www.gao.gov/fraudnet/fraudnet.htm E-mail: fraudnet@gao.gov Automated answering system: (800) 424-5454 or (202) 512-7470
Congressional Relations	Katherine Siggerud, Managing Director, siggerudk@gao.gov, (202) 512-4400, U.S. Government Accountability Office, 441 G Street NW, Room 7125, Washington, DC 20548
Public Affairs	Chuck Young, Managing Director, youngc1@gao.gov, (202) 512-4800 U.S. Government Accountability Office, 441 G Street NW, Room 7149 Washington, DC 20548

Please Print on Recycled Paper.

www.ingramcontent.com/pod-product-compliance
Lightning Source LLC
Chambersburg PA
CBHW080922290526
45795CB00007BA/2615